MINDSET
of the
MOON

Poetry & Prose

by

ThisLion   CahTame

Copyright © 2018 ThisLion CahTame

All rights reserved.

ISBN: 1981612459

ISBN-13: 978-1981612451

ABOUT THE AUTHOR

Poetry, which is often seen as feminine and passive, is generally not a go-to form of artistic expression for Caribbean men. In the hills of Gonzales, Belmont, and Laventille, Trinidad & Tobago, where Lion was raised, this is perhaps truer. The home of the steel pan, Laventille is no novice to creating beauty but such creativity is invariably steeped in machismo. It is an environment that may seem more conducive to the hammering of steel pans than the writing of poems. Yet it is in this setting that Lion carved a personal space for introspection and found his way to poetry. By putting pen to paper he began to unearth beauty beneath considerable pain and heartbreak. Writing became therapy for him, enabling him to transform undesirable circumstances into words that would help him heal. As he shared his musings on social media, it became clear that his words resonated with others especially women. His piece "Knowing How To Touch Her Without Touching Her Really Touches Her" garnered praise among many women for giving voice to things they wished men would see. The support that has continued to burgeon for Lion's work echoes the pleasure of seeing a man so comfortable with expressing gentleness, acknowledging beauty, and celebrating women. This collection "A Mindset of the Moon" explores these topics, but it also shows how even in our most challenging moments, we carry light. — Jenissa Sullivan

Humility	01
Ego	02 - 07
Karma	08
Needs vs Wants	09
Polygamy	10 - 11
Deficiency	12
Responsibility	13
Imperfections	14
Action	15
Constructive Criticism	16
Friendship	17
Caution	18 - 22
The Opportunist	23
Overwhelmed	24 - 25
Heartbreak	26 - 50
No Re-Fund	51
The Poet's Cry	52 - 53
Unrest	54 - 63
Skeletons In The Closet	64
Forgiveness	65

Unjust	66
The Healing	67 - 69
Strength	70 - 72
Miss-Understood	73 - 76
Flower Chid	77 - 80
Flower Girl	81
My Sun Flower	82
Focus	83 - 84
Inspiration	85
Devotion	86
Intentions	87 - 88
Inconsistency	89 - 90
Consistency	91 - 105
Balance	106
Cursory	107
Affirmation	108 - 109
Beauty	110 - 115
Melody	116
Harmony	117
Aura	118 - 124

Energy	125 - 129
Black Magic Woman	130 - 131
Touch	132 - 134
Bond	135 - 140
Communication	141 - 149
A New Day	150 - 151
Growth	152 - 163
Composure	164
Commitment	165
Day Dreams	166
Emotion	167 - 168
Passion	169
Loneliness	170
Cold World	171
Time	172 - 173
Saudade	174
The Longing	175 - 177
The Question	178
Next Lifetime	179
Direction	180 - 181

Solitude	182 - 189
Self Love	190 - 203
Adoration	204
Word To My Daughter	205 - 206
This Feeling	207 - 209
Love	210 - 229
Love Is Blind	230
Love Lines	231
Arab Love (ft Alia S.F.)	232
Perspective	233
Osculation	234 - 238
Sun-kissed	239
Thantophobia	240
Cerebration	241
Things I Look Forward To	242 - 243
The Perfect Couple	244
Chemistry	245
Long Distance Relationships	246 - 247
Marriage	248 - 249
Morning Sex	250

Black Love Matters	251
I'm Writing About You	252 - 254
Reflections	255 - 257
Deity	258 - 268
The Bibliophile	269
The Introvert	270 - 272
The Muse	273
The Busy Woman	274
The Thalassophile	275 - 277
The Bohemian Woman	278
The West Indian	279
Nature	280 - 281
Full Moon	282
Melanin	283
Repatriation	284 - 286
A Reminder	287 - 288
Fashion	289
Gratitude	290

HUMILITY

Humility Is The Compass
That Keeps Directing Us
To Our True Selves.

— ThisLion CahTame

EGO

Shallow Were You To Have Only Noticed The Beauty That Surfaces Her. Too Caught Up With What Her And Every Other Woman Had On Their Outside That You Didn't Realise She Held You In A Special Place On The Inside; Of Her Heart That Is. You Were Seeing Her But Never Really Got To See Her, The Real Her That Is, For Your Ego Wouldn't Let You.

— ThisLion CahTame

EGO

Most Were Just Infatuated By
Whom They Wanted Her To Be
— Slave To Their Ego At The
Cost Of Her Very Own Soul.
They Never Loved Her.
They Loved The Idea
Of Her, They Loved
Themselves.

— ThisLion CahTame

EGO

There's This Type Of Connection
Where Our Souls Converse With
Each Other Before We Could Even
Visually Realise Each Other's Existence.
Later On, Upon Physical Introduction,
It Brings About A Feeling Of Having
Met Before. Is This Deja Vu? No, It
Isn't. Our Souls Just Know Who's
Best For Us And Who's Not, Long
Before We Do — This Is Why We
Should Never Let Our Ego
Choose For Us.

— ThisLion CahTame

EGO

No Experience Was More
Frightening To Me Than
Looking Upon My Reflection
And Not Being Able To Reply
To My Subconscious When
Asked "WHO ARE YOU?"

— ThisLion CahTame

EGO

Maybe You Lost Her
Because You Needed
To Find Yourself.

— ThisLion CahTame

EGO

She Stood There Dressed In Insecurities,
Clothed In Challenges, Assembled In
What Ifs, And Attired In Trust
Issues. What Made You Think
That Her Underwear Was The
First Thing She Wanted
To Lose?

— ThisLion CahTame

KARMA

Such A Blessing It Is When
The Wrong Doing Of Others
Somehow Lead You In The
Right Direction. There's No
Better Karma Than Them
Seeing You Shed Light
From The Darkness
That They've Left
You In.

— ThisLion CahTame

NEEDS vs WANTS

If The Only Time A Man Can Hear
You Is When You Verbally Speak
To Him, Then He's Deaf To
What You Really NEED,
And Therefore Would
Only Be Able To Satisfy
You With Your WANTS.

— ThisLion CahTame

POLYGAMY

We Live In A World Where The Sky
Holds The Moon All Night Every
Night, Then Sends Her Home
Every Morning So That It Could
Entertain Another; Yet We
Wonder Why We Love
The Way We Do.

— ThisLion CahTame

POLYGAMY

A Shower Of Love Poured From Her
Heart With Intention That They
Would Dance In The Rain; But
Being The Polygamous Lover
That He Was, He Ran For
Shelter, And Left
Her In Pain.

— ThisLion CahTame

DEFICIENCY

He Loved Her With Just His
Heart, So Much That He
Barely Got Close Enough
To Touch Her Soul. Even
Though The Love Was
There, I Think This Is
Why She Always Felt
As Though Something
Was Missing.

— ThisLion CahTame

RESPONSIBILITY

One Of The Most Irresponsible Things A Man Can Do Is Place Doubt Into The Mind Of The Woman That Has Placed Her Trust In Him.

— ThisLion CahTame

IMPERFECTIONS

But I've Told You Already Though,
No Matter Who Abandons You
Because Of Your Imperfections,
Always Remember, None Is Ever
So Perfect That The Ending
Result Should Allow You To
Abandon Yourself. Just Let
Them Be; Gone That Is.

— ThisLion CahTame

ACTION

Calm Your Verbal Tone And
Let Your Actions Be So Loud
That What We Share Can
Be Felt Under My Skin.
Speak To My Soul For
A Change.

— ThisLion CahTame

CONSTRUCTIVE CRITICISM

As Men, Most Times We Despise Women That Tell Us What We Do Not Want To Hear. Truth Is, This Is Most Times The Better Women For Us.

— ThisLion CahTame

FRIENDSHIP

Sometimes Our Most Dangerous ENEMIES Are Those That Remain FRIENDS To Our WEAKNESSES While We Try To Attain GREATNESS.

— ThisLion CahTame

CAUTION

Honesty, Consistency, And Effort
Elevates Love.

Stay Away From Anyone That
Claims That They Love You
But Does Not Possess These
Attributes.

— ThisLion CahTame

CAUTION

Just Like The Ocean — Some Will Come
To The Shores Of Your Heart Attempting
To Make Ripples In It With Hope That
You Let Them In, Not Because They
Want To Be Immersed In Everything
That You Are But Simply Because
They're Fascinated By The Way
You Look On The Surface. Do
Yourself A Favour And Never
Let Them In.

— ThisLion CahTame

CAUTION

Sometimes Beauty Lies In The Eyes Of
The Beholder, Other Times Beauty
Just Lies. What's On The Outside
Doesn't Always Reflect What's
On The Inside, And Insight
Is Most Times More
Effective Than
Sight.

— ThisLion CahTame

CAUTION

Be Mindful Of The Things
You're Watering; Even
Vines Bloom Pretty
Flowers.

— ThisLion CahTame

CAUTION

Beautiful Things Hurt. God
Made Us Privy To This
When She Placed
Thorns On Roses.

— ThisLion CahTame

THE OPPORTUNIST

Like A Kite Stuck Up In A Tree — Not Because Someone Finds Their Way To You And Holds Onto You, Means They Are Meant For You. Some Are Simply Holding On Because You Were Available At The Time They Were Let Go. Their Intention Was Not To Stay, But To Weigh On You Until You Decide To Let Them Go. Don't Let People Be Stray Kites In Your Life. Shake Them Off So You Can Continue To Dance Freely In The Wind.

— ThisLion CahTame

OVERWHELMED

It's Not That I Ignore Messages On
Purpose, Or I'm So Busy Texting
Other People That I Forget To
Respond. It's Just That There
Are Times My Entire World
Gets Flooded By My Very
Own Thoughts, And I
Can't Help But Drop
Everything And Swim
In Them Until I'm
Able To Find My
Way Back To
Earth Again.

— ThisLion CahTame

OVERWHELMED

Sometimes I Feel As Though
My Day-dreams Are Where
Reality's At, And This World
We Live In, This So Called
Reality Is Nothing But A
Distraction. A Planet Bound
By Perplexity That I Have
No Means Of Getting Away
From, Other Than
Travelling On My
Own Thoughts.

— ThisLion CahTame

HEARTBREAK

Sometimes We Lose Them,
Other Times We Lose
Ourselves. Heavy
Becomes The Heart
That Has To Endure
Both.

— ThisLion CahTame

HEARTBREAK

I Once Believed That If I Dropped The
World And Gave My Time, Energy,
Love, Commitment, And Support To
One Person That It Would Naturally Be
Reciprocated, And I Would Have
No Need For The Rest Of The World
Because They Would Be Mine, My World
That Is. Journeying Taught Me That This
Isn't Always True, That No Matter What
You Give Others, Some Can Only Give You
Dishonesty, Inconsistency, Disloyalty,
Lack Of Commitment, And Pain —
Because They Can Only Be Who
They Are, And Not Who We
Want Them To Be.

— ThisLion CahTame

HEARTBREAK

She Was Somewhat Like An
Open Wound; Not Looking
For A Bandage, Nor Revenge
Towards The One That Made
Her This Way But Simply
The Strength To Pull
Herself Together.

— ThisLion CahTame

HEARTBREAK

Sometimes To Die Simply Means
To No Longer Be Able To Hold
Onto That One Person That
Makes Us Feel Alive.

— ThisLion CahTame

HEARTBREAK

Heartbreak Is A Drug That There's
No Rehabilitation For. After You've
Gotten Your First Dose Everyone
Else That Comes Into Your Life
Are Nothing But Suppressants.
You Learn To Smile Again But
You Never Truly Heal.

— ThisLion CahTame

HEARTBREAK

So Bad At Letting Go I
Bleed In Cursive.

— ThisLion CahTame

HEARTBREAK

Confessions To The Night While Being Drowned By Her Tears. Confiding In Nothing But Shadows As She Attempts To Release All Fear. Betraying Her Very Own Mind As The Pressure Peers. Asking Herself A Too Familiar Question. Why
Does Her Heart
Never Hear.

— ThisLion CahTame

HEARTBREAK

He Left Her Alone With
Nothing But Excuses
For Everything.

— ThisLion CahTame

HEARTBREAK

Her Eyes Whispered Tales Of Tragedy
Almost Every Time I Looked Into Them.
She Was Indeed Broken, Flawed, Yet
All I Was Concerned About Was
Loving Her. Never Once Did The
Thought Of Dismissing Her
Come To Mind; For Dismissing
A Woman Because She's Broken
Would Be Like Hating The Moon
When She's At Her Last Quarter—
Unworthy To Feel Her Light,
And Watch Her Shine At
Full Bloom.

— ThisLion CahTame

HEARTBREAK

Just As Water Revives The
Dehydrated, So Does Teardrops
Pitter-Patter Onto Our Skin
Attempting To Wake Our Souls
From Slumbering In Places
Where Love Won't Grow.

— ThisLion CahTame

HEARTBREAK

It's The Things That Burn
That End Up Shedding
The Brightest Light.
Stars, Galaxies,
Heartbroken
Women.

— ThisLion CahTame

HEARTBREAK

To Have Been Hurt Means To Have
Believed There Was Another Way —
Only To Be Shaken By Reality In
Its Attempt To Wake Us Up From
A Nightmare Dressed Up In The
Form Of A Dream. A Dream We
Had No Intention Of Waking Up
From — The Aching Resignation
Of Having To Accept That Their
Character Flaw Could Not,
And Would Never Change.

— ThisLion CahTame

HEARTBREAK

We've All Been Broken. It's
What We Do With The
Pieces That Are Left
Of Us That
Matters.

— ThisLion CahTame

HEARTBREAK

When You Left I Emotionally Returned
To That Time And Place In Search Of
All My Mistakes. Indeed I Did Find
Them. Some Burnt Me, Most
Taught Me, But All Punctured
A Part Of Me I Was Never Able
To Hold Physically Yet Give
Abundantly. Only Then
Was I Truly Conscious
Of What You Felt Like.

— ThisLion CahTame

HEARTBREAK

Like Rain Clouds — We Have
All Experienced What It
Feels Like To Lose Hold
Of Oneself Just To
Nurture Another.

— ThisLion CahTame

HEARTBREAK

Heartbroken So Much That I Despise
Mornings And Have Lost All Interest
In The Noon. I've Got It So Bad That
I'm Afraid Of The Evening, And
Jealous Of The Moon. Jealous
Of How Lucky She Is To See You
Sleep At Night. Envious Of Her,
For Even At The Darkest Hour,
Unlike Myself, She Would Still
Be Able To Grant You Light.

— ThisLion CahTame

HEARTBREAK

Like Scattered Seeds — Maybe
We're Supposed To Break
Before We Blossom.

— ThisLion CahTame

HEARTBREAK

All You Gave Me Were More
Reasons To Add Brick To My
Wall And Confirmation
That I Should No Longer
Wear My Heart On My
Sleeves.

— ThisLion CahTame

HEARTBREAK

Intense Sadness Could Be Seen
In Her Eyes As She Peered
Through Her Own Tears
And Saw His Lies. It Was
The First Time She Found
Revelation In Her Cries.
Relationship Ended.
Falsified Lover
Undisguised.

— ThisLion CahTame

HEARTBREAK

In Regards To Heartbreak,
Intuition Has Always Been
Our Window To Tomorrow,
But We Continuously Lie
To Ourselves By Always
Dismissing What It
Shows Us.

— ThisLion CahTame

HEARTBREAK

The Beach Was Her Last Resort. She Sat There, Cried, Then Her Attention Was Drawn To The Sea And Its Shore. It Reminded Her Of Her Relationship. He Was The Sea, Taking Pieces Of Her, The Shore, Every Time He Came And Go. Leaving Nothing Of Value With Her, Or Anything That Would Magnify Her Beauty; Only His Debris And Everything Else That Served Him No Purpose.

— ThisLion CahTame

HEARTBREAK

Too Many Times We've Placed Our
Hearts In The Hands Of Strangers
For Nothing But Mere Possibility
And Expectations. Too Consumed
With What We Want Out Of
Them That We Fail To Take
The Time To Let Them
Reveal Their Truth So
We Would Be Conscious
Of What They Really
Want From Us.

— ThisLion CahTame

HEARTBREAK

I Never Understood Why
Wolves Cry Until I Was
No Longer Able To
View The Moon In
Your Eyes.

— ThisLion CahTame

HEARTBREAK

When Some Physically Leave,
Mentally They Never Do. It
Then Goes On To Be The
Hardest Part Of The Relationship,
For After All This Time We Only
Now Realise That They Were
Always Residing Within Us.

— ThisLion CahTame

HEARTBREAK

Spent My Life In The Warm Comfort Of Your Light Until The Darkness Of Your Solitude Returned In The Form Of My Own Reflection. Now I Know What Being Blinded By Light Feels Like; For I Walk Around Guided By Pain Instead Of A Walking Cane. Growing Much More Insane, For The Only Image I Can Recall Is Your Beautiful Face Which Haunts Me Daily And Makes My Tears Fall Like A Thunderous Rain. Making My Burden Heavier Everyday, For No Longer Do I See The Light As I Search For Nothing Else But The Right Drug For This Pain, Elements C_{13} H_{20} N_2 O_2, Otherwise Known As Procaine.

— ThisLion CahTame

NO RE-FUND

Gave Up The Soul For A Mate, And
Lost The Heart. My Mind Still
Belongs To Me, But These
Abhorrent Thoughts Keep
Tearing Me Apart. Harp
Songs I've Clung To, Not
Much Interest Lays In
The Beat Of The Drum
And Bass. My Angels And
Demons Have Acquired
Such An Idiosyncratic
Taste.

— ThisLion CahTame

THE POET'S CRY

Beloved, These Words Are Homeless Without You. What Were Paragraphs Are Now Merely Broken Sentences — For Poet Without Muse Is What My Jail Sentence Is. The Metaphors May Have Been Released From Mind To Papyrus But That's Just The Same As Allowing Prisoners To Use The Gym; For Even Though They Exercise And Do What They Love, It's Still Within Those Walls Around Them. Those High Walls Somewhat Like The Ones Placed Around My Heart, That I Have No Intention Of Ever Breaking Down, Because You'd Appreciate Me More If You Were The One That Fought A Bit For Us To Be A Part. A Part And Not Apart, For It's The Nature Of The Gemini In Me To Show Not All, But Seclude These Parts Of Me That I Hide. Segregation Of Self That I Can Never Seem To Place Together Without Making

Other Things Collide. Maladroitly Yet
Unintentionally Messing Up Things
Once In A Blue Moon, Yet The Sentence
For It Goes On For More Than Just
One Afternoon. More Than Just An
Afternoon, As A Matter Of Fact
More Than Just One Night Or Day.
Sentenced To Write Sentences For
I Can No Longer Call It Poetry
Because The Fuel For My
Inspiration Which Is
Known As My Muse
Has Gone Away.

— ThisLion CahTame

UNREST

I Would Sell What's Left Of My
Soul To Get A Glimpse Of What's
On Your Mind. If I Found Out
That Beautiful Untold Thoughts
Of Me Reside There Then
It Would Be Worth It; For
Not Knowing How You Feel
Haunts Me More Than
Any Other Entity Ever
Did.

— ThisLion CahTame

UNREST

These Scars Are Slowly Healing,
But The Memory Of
WHAT ONCE WAS
Cuts Deeper Than
The Sharpest
Of Blades.

— ThisLion CahTame

UNREST

As A Child I Wish My Parents
Told Me They Loved Me More
But Most Importantly I Wish
They Loved Each Other In
My Presence
More.

— ThisLion CahTame

UNREST

Daylight Now Hurts But It's
Nothing Compared To The Night.
Unrest And Non Bottled Emotions,
Along With Thoughts Of What's
No Longer Within Sight.

— ThisLion CahTame

UNREST

Living Alone Doesn't Necessarily Guarantee Peace And Quiet. Sometimes Silence Speaks Louder Than Anything Else In This House Where I'm Constantly Haunted By Memories Of You And I. Pillows Are No Longer Comforting, For The Things They Whisper Into My Ears Makes Sleep Hard To Find. Mirrors Talk Too Much And Wardrobes Are Now Filled With Feelings That No Longer Fit Me. Home Isn't Always Home.

— ThisLion CahTame

UNREST

The Dreams Still Continue
Even Though I'm Awake;
Unfortunately The
Nightmares Too.

— ThisLion CahTame

UNREST

When My Mind's Not At Peace The
Journey To Find Sleep Can Be So
Much Hell. I Lay Listening To
The Screams Of Silence And The
Uncanny Stories They Tell. One
Eye Open, Looking Somewhat Like
An American Dollar Bill, For In
God We Trust. Staring Through
The Flames Of Fire Yet Being
Burnt By Nothing But Reality,
For Attendance Of Life's
Lessons Is Always
A Must.

— ThisLion CahTame

UNREST

The Pain She Was Dealing With
Gained More Ownership Of Her
Than She Had Of Herself; So
Much That She Became
Unavailable To The Rest
Of The World. Away From
Consolation From Others
But Even More Sadly
From Her Own Self.

— ThisLion CahTame

UNREST

Forever Haunted, Rest Wanted. Sleep
Arrives In The Form Of Slumber
And It's There I Find Myself
Malaised In Somnambulism;
Searching All Night For The
Chords Of My Heart's Broken
Melody That's Lost In Between
Shrieks, Cries, And Sighs.
Such A Perpetual Demise.

— ThisLion CahTame

UNREST

The Arms Of Danger Seem So
Inviting When You're Tired
Of Embracing Your Own Soul.
The Consequences No
Longer Matter; For Hope
Has Already Been Shattered,
And Pain Is Accepted Rather
Than That Numb Feeling
Of Being Alone.

— ThisLion CahTame

SKELETONS IN THE CLOSET

I Envy Those That Had Or Still
Manage To Hide Skeletons In
Their Closets; For Throughout
My Life I've Never Been Able
To Contain Any Of Mine.

— ThisLion CahTame

FORGIVENESS

Give Yourself Another Chance.
You're Deserving Of Your
Own Forgiveness
More Than That
Of Anyone Else.

— ThisLion CahTame

UNJUST

Morning Dew Is Proof That Even
The Moon Cries. I Would Too If
I Had To Leave You Every
Morning, Knowing That
Someone Else Will Soon
Be Here To Kiss Your
Body Throughout
The Day.

— ThisLion CahTame

THE HEALING

Woman, Even Though You've
Been Broken You've Still Got
The Power Manifested Within
You To Build The Perfect
You. You're A Creator,
So Go Create Her.

— ThisLion CahTame

THE HEALING

Poets, Artists, Introverts, And Misfits
— We WRITE OUR WRONGS And
Reflect On Them In Order To
RIGHT OUR WRONGS. It's
More Than Just Putting Pen
To Paper. This Is How We
Evolve. This Is How
We Heal.

— ThisLion CahTame

THE HEALING

Mental Menstruation— Because Thoughts Of You Deserve No Place In My Mind.

— ThisLion CahTame

STRENGTH

Free Yourself From Whatever
You're Dealing With, But
Take The Lesson
With You.

— ThisLion CahTame

STRENGTH

Find The Sunset, Take A
Good Look At It — That
Right There Is Proof
That Even Though
You're Burning
You're Still
Beautiful.

— ThisLion CahTame

STRENGTH

Even The Most Delicate Flower
That Has Been Walked Over,
Manages To Find The
Strength To Rise And
Bloom Again.

— ThisLion CahTame

MISS-UNDERSTOOD

There's An Old Book Where
Her Heart Is Supposed To
Be, And It's Yet To Be
Translated.

— ThisLion CahTame

MISS-UNDERSTOOD

Like A New Book On A Shelf,
Not Because You've Held Me,
And I've Opened Up To You,
Means That You Know
My Story.

— ThisLion CahTame

MISS-UNDERSTOOD

She's Well Written.

Most Are Just Too
Illiterate To Read
Between Her
Lines.

— ThisLion CahTame

MISS-UNDERSTOOD

I'm Interested In All Of You, Not
Just The Happy Side. I Want The
Side Nobody Ever Listens To,
The Side Everyone Thinks Need
Fixing. Not To Fix It But To Show
Them That Nothing Was Ever
Wrong With It, And That They
Never Took The Time To Read
Your Manual. In Other Words,
I Truly Want To Take The
Time To Overstand You.

— ThisLion CahTame

FLOWER CHILD

Colours Of Brown, Colours Of Blue. Flower Child, Everyone Is Always Amazed When Their Eyes Are Placed Upon You. Your Colours Are So Vivid, Oh How They Love Your Hue; But Does Anyone Ever Really Notice The True Colours Of You? Some See Aggravation But You My Dear Are Aggregation. Yes Aggregation, For Even Though It's All Love, Not All Are Wise Enough To Overstand The Perceptions Of Love That Your Atoms Bear; Forever Finding Fault In These Bright Colours Of Hair That You Wear. Little Do They Know That It's A True Representation Of All The Wisdom, Innovation, And Passion You've Got Going On In There. It's Not Just About Physical Attributes, It's Not Just About Your Lovely Scent. It's The Way You Bend And Not Break, Or Be Weathered By The Storm As If Your Stems And Roots Are Earthed In Cement.

"SHE'S SO PRETTY, WHY DOESN'T SHE ALWAYS SMILE?" Have Been Heard From The Lips Of A Few. The Lips Of A Few That Know Not That Smiles Are Something More Than Just A Physical Expression Worn On The Outside Of You. Smiles Are Celebrations, Internal, And Not Only An External Expression Of A Mouth But A Great Feeling Inside When You Know What You're About. Flower Child With You I Have No Doubt When It Comes To You Knowing What You're About, For It Seems That You Have Always Been Surrounded By Positivity Ever Since You Were Just A Sprout. Even Before You Were A Sprout, When You Were Merely Just A Seed We Were Able To Tell That You Were Here Not Just To Occupy A Space While Looking Beautiful In It But To Make A Mark In The Universe And Succeed.

Now You're No Sprout Anymore. You're All Grown Up, Most Importantly Prayed Up. Always Showing Gratitude To God, This Is Why You Stay Up. Yet While You Stay Up Some Just Wanna See You Down. But This Will Never Happen, For Your Roots Are Firmly Planted In The Ground. Firmly Planted In The Ground Even Though Most Times You're Always Surrounded By Water. You've Always Been A Perfect Representation Of Oshun's Long Lost Daughter. Shades Of Purple Around Your Neck Worn Like A Necklace To Represent Sensitivity And Care. Bits Of Green Around Your Eyes, An Epitome Of Growth, Peace, And Harmony With Nature, Of Which You Generously Share. Always Showing Love, Flower Child You're Always Showing Light, Yet Some Take Your Kindness For Weakness And Will Try Anything To Get A Bite. Thinking That They Can Kiss Your Lips In Hope To Taste Your Petals When They're Not

Even Worthy To Taste Your Truth. As A Matter Of Fact They Can't Even Touch Your Fruit, And The Only One That's Worthy Of Receiving Your Kisses Right Now Is Mother Nature, For She's Not Just The Only One That Knows You But Is Also The One Responsible For The Colours Of Your Truth.

— ThisLion CahTame

THE FLOWER GIRL

When You Have First Laid Eyes On Her,
Be Smart Enough To Know That You
Should Not Touch Her, And Respect
Her Enough Not To Try To Pick Her
Upon Sight. Just Be Confident;
Know That If Your Energy Is
Strong Enough She Will Lean
Towards You Just As She
Does Towards The Sun,
And As Long As You Keep
Sharing This Energy With
Her, Being The Flower That
She Is, She Will OPEN UP
To You.

— ThisLion CahTame

MY SUN FLOWER

She Ain't A Rose. She Ain't A Rose But I Love Her Enough To Bow Down And Kiss Her Toes. To Stand Beside Her No Matter What A New Day Shows. To Walk Beside Her As She Picks Her Fro. To Demonstrate How I Feel About Her So The Entire Universe Knows. To Taste The Marijuana On Her Lips As The Holy Sacrament Burns Slow. To Make Every Second Count In Between The Time She Comes And Goes. She Ain't A Rose. No She Ain't A Rose But She'll Always Be My Favourite Flower. For When She's Around She Feeds My Soul And Not My Ego Power.

— ThisLion CahTame

FOCUS

May My Will Power To Execute What's **NEEDED** Always Be Stronger Than My Urge For The Things I **WANT**.

— ThisLion CahTame

FOCUS

If You're Losing Sleep, Make
Sure It's For Something That's
Going To Build You, And Not
Over Someone That's
Constantly Trying To
Break You.

— ThisLion CahTame

INSPIRATION

Fill My Mind With Oil.

Feed The Fire Therein
So That My Dreams
May See Their Way.

— ThisLion CahTame

DEVOTION

You Were The Language He Never
Learned To Speak, That One Book
That Laid On His Bedside That He
Never Took The Time To Read,
The Library He Could Never
Make It To Before Closing
Time. The Problem Was
Never You — But His
Dedication Towards
All The Things That
Made You You.

— ThisLion CahTame

INTENTIONS

You've Got Good Intentions,
But Good Intentions Without
Action Is Just Admiration,
And Admirers Are Something
I Have Enough Of.

— ThisLion CahTame

INTENTIONS

She Never Wanted The World;
Just Someone That Was Crazy
Enough To At Least Make
An Attempt To Give It
To Her.

— ThisLion CahTame

INCONSISTENCY

People With Lips That Speak
Louder Than Their Hearts
Do — Usually Have
Nothing Good
To Offer.

— ThisLion CahTame

INCONSISTENCY

Rid Yourself Of Those That Show No Interest In All Of You. The Ones That Tolerate Your Soul Just To Be With Your Body.

— ThisLion CahTame

CONSISTENCY

I Presented Her With Consistency
Rather Than Roses — Because
She Deserved Something
That Wouldn't Wither
After A Period Of Time.

— ThisLion CahTame

CONSISTENCY

If Granted The Opportunity,
Be So Godly That You're Able
To Create Butterflies In Her
Stomach, Yet So Consistent
That They May
Never Leave.

— ThisLion CahTame

CONSISTENCY

Most Times It's Patience That
Builds The Room Needed For
Her To Let You In, And
Consistency That Makes
Her Comfortable Enough
To Show You Who She
Really Is.

— ThisLion CahTame

CONSISTENCY

Girl, Don't You Know That It's
The Ones That Are Consistently
Contented With Just Walking
The Shores Of Your Aura That
Will Be Grateful To Be Immersed
In Your Existence. There Are
Levels To This — You Can't
Keep Allowing People That
Aren't Even Aware Of The
Shade Of Your Sand To
Be All Up In Your
Waters.

— ThisLion CahTame

CONSISTENCY

Care And Consistency
Towards What Matters,
Would Create A Bond
Stronger Than Any
Physical Matter.

— ThisLion CahTame

CONSISTENCY

I Wanna Be Yours. I Want
Us To Belong To Each Other,
Work Together, Grow Together,
Strip Each Other Of The Cloak
Of 'WHAT IFS' That We've
Been Wearing, And Clothe
Each Other In Nothing But
Love And Light.

— ThisLion CahTame

CONSISTENCY

I'm In Love With The
Melody Of Your Soul;
Keep It Consistent
With Me, And You'll
Always And Forever
Be My Favourite
Song.

— ThisLion CahTame

CONSISTENCY

Be That Sensual Secret Her
Mind Never Forgets, And
You'll Be That Puissant
Passion Her Body And
Soul Forever Hungers
To Behold.

— ThisLion CahTame

CONSISTENCY

Place My Existence In The
Bosom Of Your Being. Let
EVERYTHING That
I AM Surrender To
EVERYTHING
That You Are.

— ThisLion CahTame

CONSISTENCY

It's Not That I Mind Giving My Love To
Someone That Comes And Goes. It's
Just That In The Process, If You're
Not Going To Be Like The Sun And
Caress My Body With Kisses Until
My Perspiration Gives Praises To
Your Presence, Or Walk With Me
And Show Me The Way In The
Darkest Of Times Like The
Moon Does, You'll Just
Be A Waste Of
My Time.

— ThisLion CahTame

CONSISTENCY

Give Her A World So Beautiful
That She'll Have No
Intention Of Returning
To The One That
She's Accustomed
To.

— ThisLion CahTame

CONSISTENCY

I AM HERE TO STAY.
The Only Thing I'll Be Leaving Is
My SCENT On Your PILLOWS,
My TASTE On Your LIPS,
A SMILE On Your FACE,
My LOVE In Your HEART,
And ASSURANCE
That We'll Never
Be Apart.

— ThisLion CahTame

CONSISTENCY

So High I Might Just Put A
Semi Colon On The Moon
For You. When You See
It Know It's Because I
Have No Intention Of
Letting This Night
End.

— ThisLion CahTame

CONSISTENCY

Love Her Like You Didn't
Have Another Option,
Like She Was All That
Existed. Carefully Yet
Consistently Tend To
What You Both Share,
And See It Bear Fruit
Rather Than
Face Extinction.

— ThisLion CahTame

CONSISTENCY

I'm Just Trying To Keep Our Love
Like Brand New By Never Getting
Too Comfortable; For Comfort
Leads To Complacency, And
Seeing That Complacency Is
Synonymous With Egotism,
I Ain't Trying To Give You
Anything That's Bad
For Your Soul.

— ThisLion CahTame

BALANCE

Start Fires In Me Only If They're
As Radiant As The Ones In Your
Eyes. Kiss Me Only If Your Lips
Can Hold Onto Me The Way
Your Hands Do. Put Butterflies
In Me Only If You're Going
To Create A Flame Bright
Enough To Attract
Moths Too.

— ThisLion CahTame

CURSORY

She Was Gorgeous Though, So
Gorgeous That Most Never
Got To See Beyond That;
For She Lived In A World
Where Image Was Everything,
Where Most Were Infatuated
By What Their Eyes Interacted
With At Surface Level — So
Much That They Never Got
To Realise How Beautiful
She Was.

— ThisLion CahTame

AFFIRMATION

I Have Yet To Meet You, But I Want
You To Know That I Am Yours. I'm
Here Waiting For You, And Our Love
Is About To Be Born. When This
Happens I Shall Take This Very
Love And Bury It Deep Into The
Soil Of The Place Where We
First Met. Not To Hide Or End
It But To Let It Take Root,
Grow, And Live To Tell A
Story Long After We
Have Physically Left
This World.

— ThisLion CahTame

AFFIRMATION

Affirmation Is Just As Important
As Prayer; Speak The Things
You Want Into Existence Just
As You Would Give Thanks
For The Ones You Have
Already Received.

— ThisLion CahTame

BEAUTY

Beauty Is When Her Aura's Equally Coalesced With Humility, Yet Still Stands Out Much More Than Her Appearance Does; Even Though She's Extremely Gorgeous.

— ThisLion CahTame

BEAUTY

Ain't Nothing As Beautiful As
A Woman Who Wants To
Make Others Feel As
Good As She Does.
For She Knows What
Goes Around Comes
Around.

— ThisLion CahTame

BEAUTY

If You're Man Enough — Go Outside
And Stare At The Last Quarter Of
The Moon. Maybe Then You May
Be Able To Understand What
Women Feel Like When
They're Silent, Not Whole,
Yet Still Remarkably
Beautiful.

— ThisLion CahTame

BEAUTY

Her Eyes— So Bright They
Make Full Moons Seem
Unimportant.

— ThisLion CahTame

BEAUTY

Everything Seems More
Beautiful When I'm
Around You; Yet
Never As Beautiful
As You.

— ThisLion CahTame

BEAUTY

Be Patient With Yourself And The
So Called Flaws That Society Have
Labelled You With; You'll Soon
Come To Realise That These
Were Never Flaws But
Beauty Misinterpreted
By Minds That Dwell
Deep Into Nothing
But Mediocrity.

— ThisLion CahTame

MELODY

Her Melody Was Everything;
Somewhat Like A Beautiful
Song, Enchanting The
Ones That Paid Attention
To What She Had To Say,
Captivating Whosoever
Was Able To Move To
Her Beat, And Appreciated
By Those That Knew A
Classic When They
Saw One.

— ThisLion CahTame

HARMONY

Place A Song In My Ribcage
But Keep The Lyrics With
You; Recite Them With
Every Breath So There'll
Always Be Harmony
Between Me
And You.

— ThisLion CahTame

AURA

I Could Care Less If The Sunset
Remains Unwritten, Or If The
Moon Decided Not To Show;
For They May Give Light To
Others, But I Find No
Mockery In Saying
That They're Nothing
Compared To Your
Glow.

— ThisLion CahTame

AURA

Forgive Them, For Not All
Are Able To See You For
Who You Really Are;
Some Are Just
Blinded By
Your Light.

— ThisLion CahTame

AURA

Of All The Things That Interest
Me, None Is More Inspiring
Than A Woman That Displays
Her Art On Her Aura. A
Masterpiece In Motion
Radiating So Beautifully
That You Fall In Love
With Her Vibe Long
Before You Even
Get To Know
Her Name.

— ThisLion CahTame

AURA

She Is Infinite; Worth Much
More Than Gold. To Be
Saturated In Her Aura —
Would Be To Feel The
Entire Universe
Within Your
Soul.

— ThisLion CahTame

AURA

Behold Her Light, The Way She
Shines, The Luminosity Of Her
Skin — That Strong Sense Of
Melanin. The Way Her Aura
Radiates The Hearts Of All
That Interact With Her,
You'd Swear She Was
The Moon's Daughter.

— ThisLion CahTame

AURA

Make Her Aura Blush Before You
Attempt To Touch Her Skin.
Make That Mental And
Spiritual Connection
Between Each Other
So Strong That Even
Your Energy Makes
Her Grin.

— ThisLion CahTame

AURA

I Love My Women Just As I Love
My Surroundings— Natural.
When I Say Natural I'm
Not Just Speaking
About Hair, But
Most Importantly
Her Presence. It
Should Bring About
A Zen Feeling Just
As Sunsets And
Full Moons Do.

— ThisLion CahTame

ENERGY

Her Skin Blushes By Just
The Mere Shadow Of My
Touch. The Closer I Get
The Brighter Her Smile.
Another Revelation
That She Loves
Me So Much.

— ThisLion CahTame

ENERGY

If Their Absence Brings About
Peace Rather Than Their
Presence — Keep Them
Out Of Your Life.

HARBOUR GOOD
VIBES ONLY.

— ThisLion CahTame

ENERGY

Give Me Nothing But Peace,
Even If That Means Staying
Away From Me.

— ThisLion CahTame

ENERGY

Come Wait For The Moon With
Me, The Sunrise Too. Let Our
Frequencies Dance Together,
Even After We're Greeted
By The Morning Dew.

— ThisLion CahTame

ENERGY

You've Taken Residence In
My Mind Even Though I
Have Yet To Hold You.
You're Welcomed To
Enter My Heart As
Well; Make Yourself
At Home.

— ThisLion CahTame

BLACK MAGIC WOMAN

Drawn To Her Because I Prefer Wise
Witches And Not Bad B*tches. Every Time
I Glance Into Her Eyes I'm Entrapped
By Her Spell, The Way Her Presence
Causes Calefaction You'd Think She's
From Hell. Not Sure Where She Resides,
But If I Had One Guess I'd Say The Dark
Side Of The Moon. Unapologetically
Dipped In Black, With A Walk That
Turns More Heads Than The Monsoon.
Lips Full Of Pleasure, A Body You'd
Love To More Than Visually Measure,
But If You Pay Attention To The
Subliminal Messages That She Feeds
You, You'd Realise That Her Mind
Is Her Greatest Treasure.

She Doesn't Do 'Real N*ggas' You Gotta
Be A God Or At least A King, Because
She Loves To Get High And I'm Not
Just Talking About Marijuana; For
Rising The Kundalini Is Her Thing.
You'd Find Her Far From The
Mediocre, Somewhere Between
The Pages Of A Book Or Where
No One Could See Her Face; For She
Knows That Beauty Lies In Mystery,
So Physical Interaction With These
Slaves Is Something She
Would Always Efface.

— ThisLion CahTame

TOUCH

Knowing How To Touch Her
Without Touching Her Really
Touches Her; This Is Something
All Should Know. She Needs
Physical Action, But Physical
Action Is Just A Mere
Fraction Of What Gives
Her Satisfaction.

— ThisLion CahTame

TOUCH

Have You Ever Kissed Her
Thoughts? Made Love To
Her Mind? Placed Images
In Her Head Of You Holding
Her From Behind? Holding
Not Just Her Body, But Her
Spirit, And Soul. Touching A
Woman Without Physically
Being There Is Beauty
To Behold.

— ThisLion CahTame

TOUCH

If I'm Not Able To Touch
You From Within, Then
I Deserve To Be Without,
You That Is.

— ThisLion CahTame

BOND

I Crave Your Entire
Being; I Wanna
Interlock Energies
With You.

— ThisLion CahTame

BOND

I Wanna Have The Pleasure Of Basking
In Your Aura While Stimulating Your
Mind So Well And Penetrating Your
Soul So Deeply, It Drives Your Body
To A State Of Jealousy — Causing It
To Hunger For The Very Stimulation
And Penetration I Would Have
Given To The Rest Of
Your Existence.

— ThisLion CahTame

BOND

We Are Nothing But Incomplete
Sentences Without Each Other,
But Together We Are The
Perfect Love Story.

— ThisLion CahTame

BOND

It Would Be Gratifying To Wrap You In My Arms Under The Moonlight Just Like The Sea Shrouds The Shore; Forever Keeping You Moist As Our Bodies Dance To The Rhythm Of Nothing But Our Very Own Heartbeats.

— ThisLion CahTame

BOND

To The Sound Of The Ocean We Shall Dance. Hand In Hand, Feet Buried In The Sand While The Sunset Watches. The Evening Wind Throttles Across One Of Your Shoulders While My Lips Parade The Other. The Only Other Music I'd Love To Hear Is Your Voice Telling Me That It's Me You Love And No Other. Palm Trees Sway Until They're Close Enough To Hold Each Other, As If They Too Are Standing In Love. In Anticipation The Night's Moon Shows Up Early As She Blushes At Us From Above. The Ocean Continues To Sing, But Its Tide Isn't The Only Thing That's Rising. The Sun Decides To Leave Because The Heat We're Giving Off Has Become Too Much For His Eyes. The Ocean Is Now Jealous, For No Longer To Its Sound Does Your Body Go, But To The Rhythm Of What I've Put Inside You As You Start Gyrating To And Fro. — ThisLion CahTame

BOND

Open Up, Unfold; The Light Within Me Yearns To Bond With That Which Is Within You.

— ThisLion CahTame

COMMUNICATION

Some Of The Finest Poetry Were
Born In The Midst Of Substantial
Conversation Between
Passionate People.

— ThisLion CahTame

COMMUNICATION

You're A Goddess, You Speak With More Than Just Your Tongue, Your Eyes Tell Your Truth Every Day, But Is He Brave Enough To Look Into Them And See What You're Saying, Or Is His Ego Just Causing Him To See His Own Reflection? Most Of The Time A Woman's Silence Speaks More Substance Than Any Man Will Ever Utter; For That's When Her Soul's Articulating. Pay Attention To Her Energy; As Costly As It May Seem, It's Nothing Compared To The Price You'll Have To Pay If You Choose Not To. A Woman's Presence, Whether It Be Physically, Spiritually, Or Mentally, Will Always Speak For Itself. Be Man Enough To Know How To Open This Present While It's In Your Presence.

— ThisLion CahTame

COMMUNICATION

Most Times Our WORDS
Are Only Appreciated By
Others When Our
SILENCE Starts
Haunting Them.

— ThisLion CahTame

COMMUNICATION

When Our Eyes Spoke Rather
Than Our Lips, And Our Souls
Listened To Each Other,
Rather Than Ours Ears Only,
It Brought About The Most
Divine Of Conversations
I've Ever Experienced.

— ThisLion CahTame

COMMUNICATION

The Right Words Whispered
To The Right Soul At The
Right Time Can Cause
The Loudest Vibration.

— ThisLion CahTame

COMMUNICATION

She Got Tired Of Repeating Herself,
Verbally That Is. So Much That Most
Times Her Energy Would Usually
Take The Forefront Of The
Interactions That Her Lips Were
No Longer Fond Of Venturing.
She Was Without Words, Yet Still
Had Something To Say; For Even
In Her State Of Silence, If
Dues Of Attention Are Paid,
And You Listen To Her
Attentively You Could
Hear Every Emotion.

— ThisLion CahTame

COMMUNICATION

Know That Even Though
I'm Silent, Thoughts Of
You Never Are.

— ThisLion CahTame

COMMUNICATION

In Her Eyes You'll Find
All The Questions Her
Lips Never Found
The Courage
To Ask.

— ThisLion CahTame

COMMUNICATION

I'm Not A Fan Of Small Talk Nor People
Who Feel That They Need To Say
Something Verbally To Get My
Attention; For I Have Seen Eyes
That Have Spoken More Substance
Than Lips Did, And That Type Of
Aberrant Behaviour Is Something
I'll Always Be Attracted To.

— ThisLion CahTame

A NEW DAY

Yesterday Died With Such Grace.
I AM Thankful For This New Day.
May Everything That Was Not
Fulfilling, Able To Add Growth
But Instead Take Away From
The Development Of Self
Rest There In Peace As Well;
For I Don't Intend To
Resurrect Them.

— ThisLion CahTame

A NEW DAY

I Hope The Morning Sings You
A Song That Keeps Your Spirits
Lifted, And That The Sun
Smiles On You
Throughout
The Day.

— ThisLion CahTame

GROWTH

Be Angered Not By The Winds
That Bring Restlessness To
Your Leaves; For They Too
Shall Scatter The Very
Seeds That Beget
Growth.

— ThisLion CahTame

GROWTH

Embrace Where You Are; Even If
You Feel As Though You're Lost
There's A Lesson To Be Learned
While You're There. Learn It,
Then You'll Be Able To Not
Only Move On But Also
Avoid Ending Up In The
Same Situation
Again.

— ThisLion CahTame

GROWTH

It's On To Outgrow People.
Grow On Girl.

— ThisLion CahTame

GROWTH

The Word On The Street Is That I'm
e-MOTION-al. I Don't Mind Though,
For I'm All About Growth And
Evolution, And That Doesn't
Happen By Being
Stagnant.

— ThisLion CahTame

GROWTH

At Times, Sometimes, Maybe Most Of
The Time, Rather Than Being Grown
Men We Choose To Be Assholes Yet
There Are Women That Genuinely
Take Time To Tend To This Chaos
Contained Within Us. It's Not
That They Have To, Or They're
Out Of Options; It's Just In
Their Nature To Nurture.
The Crazy Thing Is, Not
Every Man Is About
Growth.

— ThisLion CahTame

GROWTH

Breathe Easily,
Just Like Flowers Do.

Bloom Gracefully,
Just Like Flowers Do.

Drink Your Water And
Spend Time In The Sun,
Just Like Flowers Do.

— ThisLion CahTame

GROWTH

HIRE SELF To Find HIGHER SELF;
For You're The Only One That's
Fit For The Job.

— ThisLion CahTame

GROWTH

Evolution Is Beautiful;
May We All Flourish
Rather Than Just
Grow Older.

— ThisLion CahTame

GROWTH

They Say I've Changed; I Say
I'm Being Fulfilled By Restoration
Of A Higher Power, Creating
Freedom, And Moving Into
My True Purpose.

— ThisLion CahTame

GROWTH

She Spent So Much Time Trying
To Fit In, But That Space Could
Never Sustain Her; Only To Come
To The Realisation That She Was
Too Much Of A Woman To
Be There.

— ThisLion CahTame

GROWTH

Redundancy Can Be Draining.

Miss Me With That Over-exaggerated
Excuse For Consistency In Things
That Do Nothing For Our
Growth.

— ThisLion CahTame

GROWTH

Let Nature Take Its Course. No
Need For Us To Rush, No Need
For Things To Be Forced.
Everything Will Bloom
Beautifully, For Love
Is Our Source.

— ThisLion CahTame

COMPOSURE

She Looks Nothing Like She's Been
Through, And I Think That's Such
A Beautiful Trait. Character Stays
Intact Even After Being Taken
For Granted, Or When Others
Show Her Hate. Head Stays
Up, You'll Never See Her
Down; For She's Too
Royal To Allow Anyone
To Make Her Lose Her
Crown.

— ThisLion CahTame

COMMITMENT

Most Times I Feel You In My
Bones It's Because You've
Gone Deeper Than Under
My Skin. You Touched
My Soul. Now It's You
I Want To Forever
Have, Hold, And
Behold.

— ThisLion CahTame

DAY DREAMS

Whenever I Close My Eyes And
Think About The Things I Look
Forward To — I Can't Help But
See, Feel, And Taste You.
You're My Favourite Type
Of Daydream.

— ThisLion CahTame

EMOTION

Most Think I'm Too Emotional,
Yet My Emotions Will Forever
Be One Of My Greatest
Influences; For Man
Without Emotion Is Like
A Blank Canvas — Never
Touched By The Colours
Of Love, Pain, Or
Experience.

— ThisLion CahTame

EMOTION

Maybe The Oceans Are Just
The Moon's Tears. If So I
Appreciate Her Emotion,
For It Gives Me Faith
That One Day Someone
Will Appreciate
Mine.

— ThisLion CahTame

PASSION

Passion Is My Default
Setting; I Can't Help
But Feel Everything.

— ThisLion CahTame

LONELINESS

I Want To Belong To Someone
Rather Than Be Known By
Everyone; For Nights Get
Cold, And I Myself Deserve
To Have, To Behold, And To
Hold Onto Something
That's More Precious
Than Gold.

— ThisLion CahTame

COLD WORLD

The Chill That Occupies
Lonely Nights, And Day
To Day Interaction With
Cold-hearted People
Will Always Be A
Revelation To Me
That Hell Isn't A
Place Satiated
With Fire.

— ThisLion CahTame

TIME

Time Is Only An Illusion Until
Someone Important In Your
Life Isn't Around Anymore —
Then You'll Realise How
Real Every Second Of
The Days Of Life
Really Are.

— ThisLion CahTame

TIME

Sometimes I Wonder What Your
Hair Smells Like. Other Times I
Wonder What Your Skin Tastes
Like. Most Times I Wonder
What Your Thoughts Be
Like. Of All The Things I
Wonder, Nothing Visits
My Mind More Than
That Internal Question
To Self, Of What May
Have Been If I Had
Approached You At
An Earlier Time
In Life.

— ThisLion CahTame

SAUDADE

I Don't Always Sleep Alone;
Sometimes I Dream And I
Find You, But When I
Awake And You're Not
Here It's Nothing
More Than A
Nightmare.

— ThisLion CahTame

THE LONGING

And Seeing That Somehow
You've Already Managed To
Make Yourself A Necessity
To My Life, Time Away
Can Sometimes Be A
Challenge, And Not
Just Gradual Rotations
Of A Clock That Makes
The Heart Grow Fonder.

— ThisLion CahTame

THE LONGING

Flipping Through Pages Of Old
Journals, And Reminiscing On
Good Times Of Past Relationships,
With Hope That Someday I'll
Find Someone That Will Stay
Permanent As The Ink Did
When It Met These
Pages.

— ThisLion CahTame

THE LONGING

Homesick For A Place I've Never Been, For A Touch I've Never Felt, A Place Where The Taste Of The Air Alone Would Be Enough To Satisfy A Thousand Souls. Where Both Light And Darkness, Along With Silence, Solitude, And Serenity, Would All Be Synonymous In My Reality; For Not All That Are Born Make It Home. Some Die At Birth While Others Wake Up Everyday Without Even Knowing What's The True Meaning Of Living As They Roam This Earth. I Hope That One Day They Can Come To The Realisation That This Isn't So Different Compared To The Ones That Have Been Buried At Birth.

— ThisLion CahTame

THE QUESTION

What If You Found Out That This
Heart Longs For You? That Every
Beat Is An Abbreviation Of Your
Name — Calling You 86400
Times Per Day, With Hope
That You Would Answer.
Would You Hold My Name
In Your Heart Just As I've
Done Yours, Until It Not
Only Beats In Synchronisation
With Mine But Also Becomes
Mine?

— ThisLion CahTame

NEXT LIFETIME

In The Next Life I Wish To Be
The Sun, And Have Hope That
You Would Return As The
Earth — Just So I May
Appear After The Rain
To Kiss The Waters
That Has Moistened
The Petals Of Your
Flower The Very
Way I Did When
We Were Lovers.

— ThisLion CahTame

DIRECTION

Don't Go Out Of Your Way So
Much For Others That You
End Up Losing Your
Own Path.

— ThisLion CahTame

DIRECTION

The Easy Road Is Most Times
The Safest; But Nothing Is
Learnt There.

— ThisLion CahTame

SOLITUDE

Nature Have Always Taught Me
That None Is Braver Than The
Caterpillar; Admirable Is Her
Ability To Drop The World,
With Hope Of Reaching Her
True Potential; A Task That
Even Men Have Yet
To Perfect.

— ThisLion CahTame

SOLITUDE

Sometimes The Answers Hides
Within The Silence; Yet The
Silence Speaks So Loud
That It's Hard To
Differentiate
What It's
Saying.

— ThisLion CahTame

SOLITUDE

I'm A Lover Of My Own Company.
I Learn A lot More When I'm By
Myself Than When I'm In Crowds.
I'm Not Saying That Crowds Don't
Teach Me Anything, Most Times
They Show Me Who I Need Not
To Be Around. The Funny Thing
Is I've Managed To Learn That
Very Lesson From Afar.

— ThisLion CahTame

SOLITUDE

Stay In Your Zen;

Know The Difference
Between The Ones
That Come Knocking
To Join You, And
The Ones That Come
Knocking To Disturb
You.

— ThisLion CahTame

SOLITUDE

No Company Is Sometimes
The Best Company; I Find
Pleasure In Spending Time
Alone.

— ThisLion CahTame

SOLITUDE

SOLITARY CONFINEMENT?

I'm An Introvert,
Don't Threaten Me
With A Good Time.

— ThisLion CahTame

SOLITUDE

No One Can Rejuvenate Me
Like I Do; So Understand
That Getting The Best Of Me
Will Sometimes Require A
Little Less Of Me. Solitude
Builds Me, Staying
Away Too Long From
It Kills Me.

— ThisLion CahTame

SOLITUDE

Fall In Love With Solitude First;
For If You Can't Love Yourself
There You Would Never Be
Ready To Love Anyone Else.

— ThisLion CahTame

SELF LOVE

I Choose Love — And By
That I Mean Putting
Myself First.

— ThisLion CahTame

SELF LOVE

Loving Yourself First Is
Essential To Everything
You Attract, Including
The Love You Receive.
You'll Always Be
Without If It
Isn't Within.

— ThisLion CahTame

SELF LOVE

It's Ok To Be Selfish With Your Energy; It Wasn't Made For, Nor To Be Compatible With Everyone.

— ThisLion CahTame

SELF LOVE

Don't Be A Stranger To Yourself; Check For Yourself Just As You Would Check For Others. Invest Time In Yourself Just As You Would Invest Time In Others.

YOU ARE YOUR FIRST RESPONSIBILITY.

— ThisLion CahTame

SELF LOVE

Be Kind To Your Intuition;
It Only Wants What's
Best For You.

— ThisLion CahTame

SELF LOVE

Reserve Some Of The Love In
You For Days That Seem As
Though There's None
Around You.

— ThisLion CahTame

SELF LOVE

Be A Tree — Stand Your Ground,
Dance In The Wind Daily, And
Shake Off Anything That's
Not Essential To Your
Growth.

— ThisLion CahTame

SELF LOVE

Let's Teach Our Children To Love
The Skin They're In; That They're
Beautiful, And Every Time They
Feel The Sun Against Their
Skin, That Those Are
Kisses To Constantly
Remind Them That
The Heavens Are
In Love With
Everything
That They
Are.

— ThisLion CahTame

SELF LOVE

Put Some Respect On Your Worth.
Stop Giving Your Time, Energy,
Support, And Love, To Those
That Are Too Selfish
To Reciprocate It.

— ThisLion CahTame

SELF LOVE

Be Kind To Yourself. In Regards
To Love — Don't Give To
Another What You
Haven't Given To
Yourself.

— ThisLion CahTame

SELF LOVE

There's Love In Her That Lays
Dormant; Only Because It Has
Been Proven To Her On
Numerous Occasions
That Most Can't
Handle Such
A Treasure.

— ThisLion CahTame

SELF LOVE

Let Go Of Whatever Wants To Go.

Whatever Remains Show More
Appreciation To It, Even
If What Remains Just
Happens To Only
Be You.

— ThisLion CahTame

SELF LOVE

Some People LOVE OTHERS
With Ease Yet Find It Hard
To LOVE THEMSELVES.
I Pray These Souls Realise
That THEY ARE WORTHY
Of Their Own Love
First.

— ThisLion CahTame

SELF LOVE

As A Man, Respect For Women
Is Also A Form Of Self Love;
Integral Overstanding That
We Wouldn't Exist
Without Them
And Vice
Versa.

— ThisLion CahTame

ADORATION

There Are Flowers Blooming Between
Every One Of My Heartbeats And
Purpose In Every Breath That I
Breathe. The Sun's Kisses Can
Always Be Found On My Skin,
And The Moon Makes It Her
Duty To Accompany Me
Wherever I Go. I Am
Without A Doubt
Adored By The
Universe.

— ThisLion CahTame

Word To My Daughter

You Are Fine Art Displayed
On A Confidential Canvas,
Not Braille Upon Society's
Pages. No One Needs To
Touch You To Know
You How Beautiful
You Are.

— ThisLion CahTame

Word To My Daughter

Of All The Things Created By God,
I Find No Conceit In Saying That
You're My Favourite; A Wonder
Of More Than Just The
World You Are.

— ThisLion CahTame

THIS FEELING

I Just Can't Overstand This Strange Feeling
That's Inside, But It's Got Me Feeling Good,
Powerful, Romantic, And Full Of Pride.
I Just Can't Overstand This Weird
Feeling That I'm Feeling, But Whatever It Is
God Knows It's So Appealing.

Please Tell Me When Did It All Start,
From Whence It Begun.
For It Feels Like Success To Me As
Wavin' Flag Was To K'naan.
Like I Won The War, Won The Fight,
Oh Sweet Victory Is Mine,
For The Universe Has Rewarded Me Greatly
With This Someone So Divine.

Night After Night I Can't Stop Thinking
About You, Me, Us. Everything's Just Right,
No Stress, No Fight, No Fuss.
Just Kisses, Hugs And Touches,

Smiles, Grins And Blushes.
Got Me Feeling, Got Me Remembering
Those High School Crushes.
Is This What True Love Is?
Baby Tell Me That It's Real.
That It's Right, That It's Forever,
That It's Pure, Signed And Sealed.

Let Me Stop Questioning This Thing,
Let Me Be Most Thankful For This Blessing.
For If I Was To Lose This,
That Would Be A Very Painful Lesson.
They Say Love Comes From God,
I Surely See God In You.
For I Was Just Familiar With His Name,
But Never Met H.I.M. Until I Met You.
I Searched For H.I.M. In The Sky,
Left, Right, And All Different Places,
But Little Did You Know It's You That
Guided Me To Where He Really Is.

People Might Think I'm Crazy,
Some May Even Think Sprung.
But Any Woman Pushing Me Closer
To H.I.M, I'm Definitely Holding On.

So Let's Forget About Them, Those, And
They, And What They Got Say;
For The Only Person's Opinion That
Matters Is The One To Whom We Pray.
For It Was God That Created This Feeling
So If I Really Want It To Stay,
I Shall Stay Close To You So I'll Be Close To
H.I.M. For The Rest Of My Nights And Days.

— ThisLion CahTame

LOVE

Grant Me The Type Of Love Where Hearts Open Before Lips, Chakras Are Awakened Rather Than Egos, And Souls Bare Themselves To Each Other Before Bodies Do.

— ThisLion CahTame

LOVE

Surrender The Search And Let
Love Find You; That Person
May Look Good But Don't
Let What's On The Outside
Blind You.

— ThisLion CahTame

LOVE

I've Fallen For You So Hard
That It Has Already Made
Marks In My Heart And
Soul. Imprinted
You Are In Me.

— ThisLion CahTame

LOVE

Go Outside, Close Your Eyes
And Taste The Rain; That's
Heaven On Your Lips.
Whoever This Experience
Reminds You Of, Is Who
You're Truly In
Love With.

— ThisLion CahTame

LOVE

We Would Never Know Love
Until We Are Able To
Differentiate Between
Who's Leaving Footprints
In Our Heart And Who's
Just Walking
All Over It.

— ThisLion CahTame

LOVE

If I Ever Let You Into My
Heart, Promise Me That
You Would Never Take
The Lights Off.

— ThisLion CahTame

LOVE

Sooner Or Later Something Is
Going To Consume Us; We
Might As Well Give Love
The Upper-hand.

— ThisLion CahTame

LOVE

Effort Is A Main Ingredient
In Love; If There's No Effort
It Isn't Love.

— ThisLion CahTame

LOVE

Feeling Things
Some Only
Dream
Of.

— ThisLion CahTame

LOVE

It's Not That I'm Not Interested.
It's Just That With Eyes That
Beautiful, Sometimes It's Hard
For Me To Pay Attention To
What Your Lips Are Saying;
For When I Look Into Them
I Can't Help But Drift Away To
A Place Further In Time
Where I See Us Both.
I See My Future In
You, Literally.

— ThisLion CahTame

LOVE

The Best Way Of Reminding Her
How Beautiful She Is — Is NOT
By Directing Her To The Mirror,
Nor By Telling Her But By
Simply Being A Reflection
Of The Love That
She Bestows
You.

— ThisLion CahTame

LOVE

Love is Supposed To Remind
You To Breathe— This Is Why
Every Time You See Her
Your Breath Is Taken
Away.

— ThisLion CahTame

LOVE

With Lips That Taste Like Forever,
And Eyes That I See My Future In,
There's No Doubt That You're All
I Have Ever Needed; For There
Are Those That Offer The World,
But Only You Have Managed To
Make Me Feel The Entire
Universe From Within.

— ThisLion CahTame

LOVE

Love Is The Only
Language;

Everything

Else

Is

Just

Noise.

— ThisLion CahTame

LOVE

Deafen Me So I'll No Longer
Hear The Sounds Of This
Envious World; Just The
Rhythm Of Our Hearts
Beating Together As
One Is All I Need.

— ThisLion CahTame

LOVE

To Love You As Though I've
Never Been Heartbroken
Is To Give You More
Than I Gave Another;
Indeed This Is What
You Deserve.

— ThisLion CahTame

LOVE

And If God Took A Few Days To
Create The World, Yet All It Took
For Us To Fall In Love Was A
Moment, It Just Goes To Show
That Our Love Isn't Only Not
Of This World But Also A
Force To Be Reckoned
With.

— ThisLion CahTame

LOVE

I'll Take You As You Are, I'll Take
Everything That You Are And
Give You More; For It's
Both The Good And Bad
In You That I Adore.

— ThisLion CahTame

LOVE

Stand In Love With Me, I'll Write
You Into My Words; For Even If
Our Worlds Perish We'll Remained
Tattooed Into Pages For Other
Couples To See That Beautiful
Things Do Last. We May
Physically Die, But Our
Love Will Always Be
Immortal.

— ThisLion CahTame

LOVE

Love Is Lovely. You Don't Need
Another To Be Lovely. Just Be,
Lovely That Is. Be In Love,
For Love Is In You.

— ThisLion CahTame

LOVE IS BLIND

How Can Love Be Blind When It Makes
You See Someone Like No Else Could?
Do Things For Them That No One Else
Would. Go All Out For Them Because
You Think No One Else Should. Then
Again, As I'm Writing This I'm Starting
To Believe That The Term 'LOVE Is BLIND'
Is True — For In A World Filled With So
Many, Everything Else Comes Across
Blurred, And I'm Only Able To
Focus On You.

— ThisLion CahTame

LOVE LINES

Every Time I Kiss Your Scars And
Your Love Lines It's A Reminder
To You That They're Beautiful,
And That Marks Aren't Only
Physical; For You Have
Imprinted Permanent Ones
In My Soul And I'm Proud
Of Them Just As I Am
Of Yours.

— ThisLion CahTame

ARAB LOVE

I Am Not Capable Of Fully Sharing Myself With You Because Inside My Heart Is A Village Of Mutes. Your Hands Can Explore Every Inch Of My Flesh And Your Lips Can Shake The Emotions In My Heart Space, But Inside My Heart Is A Village Of Mutes. This Part Of Me Cannot Speak To You In Human Form; It Only Speaks To God In Silence When My Hands Are Crossed And My Soul Is On Its Knees. — Alia SF

I Am Ok With You Not Fully Sharing Yourself With Me; But If It's Because Within Your Heart Resides A Village Of Mutes, Then I'd Be More Than Honoured To Let My Love Speak Loud Enough For The Both Of Us As We Kiss And Taste Each Other's Truth. Vibrations Being Made By Not Only The Rhythm Of Our Existence As We Pass Through The Passage Of Time, But By The Silence Of Our Egos As Our Souls Remain Divine. — ThisLion CahTame

PERSPECTIVE

It's Crazy How Love Changes Perspective.
As A Child I Was Taught That I Should
Never Play With Fire. Many Years Later,
As A Man In Love, I Realised It Had
Nothing To Do With With Matches
But Simply Never Taking The
Woman That Sets Your
Heart Afire For Granted.

— ThisLion CahTame

OSCULATION

If Love Is God And God Is Love,
Kissing Got To Be Some Sort
Of Worship. So Let It Be
Known That Whenever
My Lips Come Into
Interaction With
Any Part Of Your
Body, I'm Just
Giving
Praises.

— ThisLion CahTame

OSCULATION

A Kiss Is Never Fully A Kiss
Until It Lingers In Your
Brain; Every Day And
Night Until You're
Able To Interact
With The Lips Of
That Significant
Other Again.

— ThisLion CahTame

OSCULATION

Kiss Her Along Her Depths,
Taste Her Inner Beauty,
Make Her Soul Ovulate.

— ThisLion CahTame

OSCULATION

Kiss Me Before The Sun Sets
While Our Bodies Bask In
The Warmth Of The Sunset.
Eyes Closed, Fingers Entwined,
Sharing All That's Devine.

— ThisLion CahTame

OSCULATION

Lips Perched Upon Your
Forehead Gently As A
Butterfly Onto A
Sunflower So That
Your Smile May
Take Flight.

— ThisLion CahTame

SUNKISSED

Take A Look At Her Complexion, So
Enchanting. Maybe She's The Reason
Why The Sun Rises; Having Once
Kissed Her Skin And Couldn't
Help Return Every Morning To
Satisfy His Lips With What He
Dreams About Every Night.

— ThisLion CahTame

THANTOPHOBIA

I Still Tremble By Your Kisses;
Not Because I'm Anxious, But
In Fear That I'd Wither If The
Moisture From Your Lips
Was To Ever Cease From
Touching Mine.

— ThisLion CahTame

CEREBRATION

Your Scent Still Lingers On
My Mind, And The Thought
Of Your Smile Is More Than
Just A Casual Visitor.
I'm Forever Thinking
About You.

— ThisLion CahTame

THINGS I LIKE FOWARD TO

Evenings Where I Place The Sunset
In Your Eyes, The Sand Under
Your Feet, The Sea On Your
Skin, And You In My Arms
— Until The Moon Herself
Appears To Remind Us
Of How Much Time
We Have Been
Spending With
Each Other.

— ThisLion CahTame

THINGS I LOOK FORWARD TO

I Wanna Have The Pleasure Of Looking
Into Your Eyes Until The Sun Comes
Up; Then I Would Have Known
What It Feels Like To
Experience Two Sunrises
On The Same Morning.

— ThisLion CahTame

THE PERFECT COUPLE

While Admiring Nature I've Come To The Realisation That I'm In Need Of The Type Of Relationship The Full Moon And The Ocean Has. I Think They're The Perfect Couple. They're Totally Different Yet They Reflect Each Other's Existence Perfectly; So Much That Even In The Darkest Hour The Ocean Still Manages To Make The Full Moon Blush, For When She Looks At Him She's Always Reminded Of How Beautiful She Is.

— ThisLion CahTame

CHEMISTRY

Forever Reserving Sunsets For You,
Evenings At Restaurants, Table For
Two. Mornings Where We Would
Watch The Moon Leave With Not
Only Its Light, But A Memory Of
What Happens When Our Bodies
Ignite. Windows Deliberately Left
Open To Show Her And The Stars
The Chemistry That Burns Between
You And I, So They Could Make It
Known To The Heavens That The
Greatest Fire Is No Longer The
One That Burns In
The Sky.

— ThisLion CahTame

LONG DISTANCE RELATIONSHIPS

And If The Rains Could Travel All The
Way From The Heavens Just To Kiss
The Petals Of The Sunflower, Then
So Must I Cross Oceans Just To See
You; For Love Knows No Distance,
Only Diligence Towards The
Things That Keeps It Afire.

— ThisLion CahTame

LONG DISTANCE RELATIONSHIPS

HER: I Like You, I Wish You Lived Closer.

ME: You Do, You Stay On My Mind, And
Seeing That I'm An Intellectual That's
A Special Place To Be; For There Are
People That Reside In My Midst
That Have No Idea What My
Aura Tastes Like, Yet Somehow
I Manage To Feed It To You
From So Far Away.

— ThisLion CahTame

MARRIAGE

Let's Write Our Own Wedding Vows;
Let The God Within Us Speak To
Each Other With Covenants
Created By No Other Lips
But Ours.

— ThisLion CahTame

MARRIAGE

I Want Us To Get Married Barefooted,
Because I Know When I Make You My
Wife Neither Of Us Will Know What
It Would Feel Like To Walk On This
Earth Again; For We Would Have
Created Our Own Heaven, And
This Love Would Be So Strong
That Hell Would Be
Nonexistent In
Our Reality.

— ThisLion CahTame

MORNING SEX

Because Coffee Should Never Be
The First Black Thing To Make
Its Way Into Her Body
On Mornings.

— ThisLion CahTame

BLACK LOVE MATTERS

Black Woman, No One Knows How To
Create Like You Do. You Are The Precursor
Of Creation Itself; Adding Life To Any And
Everything You Physically, Intellectually
Or Spiritually Commerce With. Such A
Deiform Being You Are, To Build Without
You Would Be To Tear Down Another.
That Other Would Be No One But
Myself; And Since You're A Reflection
Of Who I AM, I'll Be Indirectly Tearing
You Down As Well. Yes, This Is My
Revelation That We Need Each
Other.

— ThisLion CahTame.

I'M WRITING ABOUT YOU

You Want Me To Write About You,
Are You Sure You Can Handle My Words;
For They Can Be So Lovely
Or They Can Be Very Absurd.
I'll Start With Your Hazel Brown Eyes
That Taught Me A lot About You.
About Your Attitude, Your Ways,
And How You're Divine And True.

You've Got The Smoothest Skin,
Like A Peach in The Morning Sun.
Lips I Want On Mine, Thats So Soft
And Sweet When We Kiss And
Come Together As One.
Your Hair Is Ever Wild,
So Thick And So Pure.
Oh My Dearest African Woman,
I Can Tell You So Much More.

Your Hips Rock To The
Rhythm Of The Wind,
That Whistles Through My Ear.
Telling Me That Your Coming,
Forever Looking Gorgeous In
Whatever You Wear.
A Smile On Your Face That
Adds Sunshine To My Life,
But When I Think About
The Reality Of Things I Sometimes
Question Making You My Wife.

I Think You Haven't Found
Yourself, And You're A Little
Lost In Dismay.
You Got Carried Away By
Your Looks, And Forgot That
Tomorrow Is Another Day.
But If You Look Yourself
In The Mirror, And Stare
Yourself In The Third Eye.

You'll Truly See That Beauty In
Which You Have Deny.
You've Forgotten About Africa,
Forgotten About God,
Do You Even Pray To The Holy One?
For You Rant, Rave, And Misbehave
Like A Hunter Without His Gun.
You Were So Holy,
Very Humble Too.
I Just Got One More Thing To Say,
"I MISS THE REAL YOU."

— ThisLion CahTame

REFLECTIONS

Who AM I? Nothing But A Reflection
Of You. The Things We Find
Interesting In Others Are Most
Times The Exact Things That
Can Be Found In Ourselves;
Sometimes Buried So Deep
Within That We Can't Help
But Be Grateful To See It
Displayed Through The
Soul Of Another.

— ThisLion CahTame

REFLECTIONS

Sometimes To See Me
Naked Simply Means
To Hear What
I've Got To
Say.

— ThisLion CahTame

REFLECTIONS

A Woman That's Been Through
Hell Can Still Give You Heaven;
But You Got To Have Some
Within You To Realise That.
Heaven That Is.

— ThisLion CahTame

Y

Be You've Never Walked On Water,
Nor Turned Water Into Wine, But You've
Loved People You've Never Met, Trusted
People You've Never Seen, And Most
Importantly Touched People You've
Never Held. Woman, What More
Will It Take For You To Realise
That You're Nothing Less Than
A Goddess?

— ThisLion CahTame

DEITY

She Was Gorgeous Though. So
Gorgeous That Most Never Got
To See Beyond That; For She
Lived In A Shallow World
Where Image Was Everything.
Where Most Got Infatuated
With What Their Eyes
Interacted With At
Surface Level; So
Much That They
Never Got To
Realise How
Beautiful
She Was.

— ThisLion CahTame

DEITY

Tonight My Lips Shall Osculate The
Vertex Of Your Centrefold So Well,
That Before You Reach Culmination
Your Outcry Shall Be "OH MY GOD!"
By Then You Would Have Better
Overstanding Of What I Meant
When I Said That I Wasn't
Human.

— ThisLion CahTame

DEITY

She's Heaven On Earth,
And Shooting Stars Are
Just Awakened Angels
Making Their Way
Back Home
To Her.

— ThisLion CahTame

DEITY

Some Say The Sun Is A God; But It's The Moon That Always Seem To Make The Heavens Cry With Joy Whenever It's Blessed By Her Presence.

— ThisLion CahTame

DEITY

So Blessed, Her Presence
Makes The Devil Feel
Uncomfortable.

— ThisLion CahTame

DEITY

Overstand That She Was Made In God's
Image And Likeness, Therefore She
Can Hit You With Lightning, Roar
Like Thunder, Make It Rain, Or
Add Sunshine To Your Life.
Whichever Attribute You
Happen To Experience Will
Most Times Be Summoned
By Your Actions
Towards Her.

— ThisLion CahTame

DEITY

If Satan Is Indeed A Man,
It Would Be Obvious That
GOD Is WOMAN; For In Their
True Nature Women Have
Always Attempted To Save
Men From The Prisons Of
Narcissism That They
Have Inflicted On
Themselves.

— ThisLion CahTame

is Her Own Masterpiece,
Art In Motion. Somewhat Like
A Canvas With Inscriptions Of
Extracts Of Edgar Allan Poe
On One Side, And Shakespeare
On The Other — Gracefully
Making Her Way Through
The Winds Of The World
Without Being Weathered;
For She Was Full Of Intellect,
And Bared A Spine As Strong
As The Novels You'd Usually
Find Her Head Buried In.

— ThisLion CahTame

DEITY

You're A King's Queen, You're No
N*ggas B*tch. You're Of Royalty,
You're Divine. Know The Power
You've Got Black Woman,
Stay True To Self And
Never Switch.

— ThisLion CahTame

il That Even When
...ed in Black And White
Her True Colours Manage To
Show; This Goddess Of
A Woman I Know.

— ThisLion CahTame

THE BIBLIOPHILE

She Had More Books That
Friends; And As Odd As
It May Seem, This
Satisfied Her.

— ThisLion CahTame

INTROVERT

There's Something Interesting
About A Mysterious Woman
— Her Abstruseness Is So
Alluring. Like It's Beautiful
To Not See Her, See Her,
And Want To See Her,
All At The Same Time.

— ThisLion CahTame

THE INTROVERT

And While Others Fluttered Around
Party Lights Like Moths Amongst
Small Flames, She Was Interested
In Bigger And Brighter Things.
The Moon Excited Her,
Sapiosexuals Delighted
Her, Good Books Incited
Her, And Ambition
Inspired Her.

— ThisLion CahTame

THE INTROVERT

She Was The Type Of Woman That Made
It Past The Veils Of Your Eyes — What
You Saw Could Never Compare To
What You Wanted To Know, About
Her That Is. She Sparked Interests,
Looked Great In The Physical,
And Mysteriously Aroused
The Mental.

— ThisLion CahTame

THE MUSE

Time Spent With Her Was Always An Investment, And Conversations With Her Were Immersed In Inspiration. I Was The Writer, But She Birthed Poetry. She Was A Muse; She Was The Substance That Created Substance.

— ThisLion CahTame

BUSY WOMAN

Gain Occupancy In The Mind Of A Busy Woman Would Mean That You've Also Gained A Place In Her Heart. Respect Her Time, For It's A Commodity That Isn't Rendered To All.

— ThisLion CahTame

THE THALASSOPHILE

A Woman That Spends A lot Of Time In The Ocean Requires Nothing Shallow, Everything About Her Is Profound. If I'm Ever Blessed To Be Loved By One I'd Constantly Penetrate The Wetness Of Her Enigma, Take Deep Dives Into The Waterfalls Of Her Conscience, And Taste Her Obscurity Until I'm Familiar With What I Never Knew Existed. I'd Treat Her Like The Mermaid That She Is.

— ThisLion CahTame

THE THALASSOPHILE

Take Her To The Beach At
Night; Massage Her Feet
While The Moonlight
Tip-Toes Across Her
Spine.

— ThisLion CahTame

THE THALASSOPHILE

Forget The Club; Let's Spend
The Night At The Beach And
Dance To The Sound Of
The Ocean.

— ThisLion CahTame

THE BOHEMIAN WOMAN

While Everyone Was Trying To Be All Fly, She Was Pleased With Being Grounded. No Matter How Many Times Her Bare Feet Visited The Seashore She Would Always Be Astounded. Her Toes Loved Tasting The Sand And Her Arms Found Delight In Hugging Trees. She Was A Bohemian Woman, And Nature Brought Her Ease.

— ThisLion CahTame

THE WEST INDIAN

If Her Attitude Is As Spicy As The
Food She Eats, Skin Is As Smooth
As A Baby's Butt Cheek, And Her
Love Goes Deeper Than Where
Whales Hide Their Secrets,
She's Probably A
West Indian.

— ThisLion CahTame

NATURE

When You Take The Time To
Notice That The Sun's Kiss Is
Stronger Than That Of Any
Human, The Trees Feed
Others Just As They Do
Themselves, And The Birds
Always Have Something
Sweet To Sing About, You'll
Realise That Nature Lives
In Love More Than
We Do.

— ThisLion CahTame

NATURE

While Admiring Nature I've Come To
The Realisation That I'm In Need Of
The Type Of Relationship The Full
Moon And The Ocean Has. I Think
They're The Perfect Couple. They're
Totally Different Yet They Reflect
Each Other's Existence Perfectly.
So Much That Even In The Darkest
Hour The Ocean Still Manages To
Make The Moon Blush; For When
She Looks At Him She's Always
Reminded Of How Beautiful
She Is.

— ThisLion CahTame

FULL MOON

Stars Smiling At Us, Jupiter Too.
Planets Orbiting, The Light Of Moon
Transcends. With My Last Wish
All I Ask Is That This Night
Never Ends.

— ThisLion CahTame

MELANIN

Be So Proud Of Your Blackness That
It Makes The Moon Curious As To
What It Is To Rise Inside You.

— ThisLion CahTame

REPATRIATION

She Doesn't Wear A Head Full Of Lyes Anymore, There It Lays In Bits And Pieces, Scattered All Over Her Bedroom Floor. She's Starting A New, Even Though Hair Has Nothing To Do With Being Royal — To Her King, His Imperial Majesty She Wants To Stay Loyal. Now She's Looking So Divine With Admiration And A Natural Shine. Oh How I Love And Admire This Sweet African Woman Of Mine.

Her Style Is Natural Yet Revolutionary Like A Black Panther Queen, Beret On Her Head And Decked In Pan-African Colours Of Ites, Black, And Green. Her Head's Always Up, About Herself She's Always Sure, Ever So Smooth, Ever So Beautiful, Ever So Royal, Ever So Pure. Ears Deaf To Sounds Of 'PSSSSSTT' And 'WHISTLES' From So Called Men. She Nuh Inna Dem Styles,

This Woman Does Her Own, For She
Set The Trends.

She Stands Her Ground Like Rosa Parks,
Got Wisdom And Style Like Michelle
Obama. Always A Lady, Always Preaching
Positivity, Avoiding Negativity And Drama.
For She's Got A Oprah Winfrey Kind Of
Heart With A Maya Angelou Kind Of Soul,
Dedicated To Her King Like Empress Mennen,
Ready To Learn The Half That Wasn't Told.
So Interested In Ethiopia's Language
That She Says 'WADADA' Instead Of
'LOVE' And Starts Her Prayer With
'Abbatachin Hoy Bessemaie Yemitnore
Simih Yekedes' When Praising The
Almighty Up Above.

Her Interests Begins To Drift. Wrong Choice
Of Words, Her Interests Are Now Guided;
For The Fuel For Her Conscience, Instincts,

And Choices, From No One But God It Is Provided. So To Her It's A Whole New Beginning, She's Under A Whole New Order, Repatriated Not By Body, But By Mind, Spirit, And Soul She Crossed The Border. Broke Away From Chains That Were On Her Mind, Adhered To A Call From The Highest Of All. Born A Different Person All Because Of Her Mindset This Black Woman Now Truly Stands Tall.

— ThisLion CahTame

A Reminder

Magical Are The Women That
Most Men Take For Granted;
For They Go On To Be The
Ones That Are Missed
The Most.

— ThisLion CahTame

A Reminder

Even The Moon Constantly Changes
Darling; And On The Nights That She
Doesn't Appear Whole She Still Manages
To Light Up The Universe. Let Her Be A
Reminder To You That No Matter How
Small Your Shine, There Are Those That
Will Genuinely Love You Because They're
Aware Of Your Potential — So Much That
They Won't Mind Waiting To See You
In Full Bloom.

— ThisLion CahTame

FASHION

Fashion Is A Disruptive Behaviour;
It Confuses People. If Everyone
Instantly Gets Why You Dress
The Way You Do, Then It
Isn't Fashion.

— ThisLion CahTame

GRATITUDE

Thank Her For The Things She Has Done, For The Things She Continue To Do, And The Things She's Been Willing To Do. Women Love To Know That The Things They're Doing Aren't Going Unnoticed.

— ThisLion CahTame

THANK YOU

First of all, I would like to thank God for giving me not only life but the power to bring this project to life as well. Secondly, I'd like to thank my daughter Haile Kaira Che. I love you very much, you are by far my greatest muse and my greatest achievement; a blessing you are. You were only 7yrs old at the time this book was written, but I have no doubt that in your adolescent days you'd find not only some form of guidance here but the ability to walk through my mind via these pages. Thirdly, I'd like to thank all my other family, friends, and creatives that helped me in some sort of fashion along this journey, even if it was just to make sure that I stayed committed to my ascension; so special thanks to Alon Burrows, Ditch Fashion, Cherisse Moe, Jenissa Sullivan, Shari Cumberbatch, Lion Twin, Relative Designs, Jeniffer Johnson, Reneisha Rodriguez, Tyoshi, Genesia Mulrain, Terrell George, and anyone that I forgot to mention. Thanks as well to my fans, this would not have been possible without you all. I love and appreciate you all so much. A Mindset of the Moon is here and it's only a start of what's to come. Last but definitely not least I'll like to say a special thank you to anyone that has done me wrong in any way; for the pain that you all have inflicted, has and will always be a driving force for my writing.   — ThisLion CahTame

Stay Connected

www.thislioncahtame.com

Instagram — **@ThisLionCahTame**

Medium — **@ThisLionCahTame**

Facebook — **ThisLion CahTame**

Twitter — **@ThisLionCahTame**

Tumblr — **@ThisLionCahTame**

Made in the USA
Middletown, DE
17 February 2019